LANRE S

MELLEXY
Through Your Eyes

Disclaimer

All the material contained in this book is provided for educational and informational purposes only. No responsibility can be taken for any results or outcomes resulting from the use of this material.

While every attempt has been made to provide information that is both accurate and effective, the author does not assume any responsibility for the accuracy or use/misuse of this information.

Acknowledgements

To my friends and family that supported this special publication, my appreciation goes to you all.

To the many critics and reviewers, I thank you for your tremendous support.

To Vyankka, I deeply appreciate you being the face of this book.

To Hope Huggs, I thank you specially for birthing the idea of this book and for coining the genre *Mellexy.*

Notable mentions for the success of this book includes Chinyere Vivian Akwuneche, Joseph Chuck Ikechukwu and everyone that supported the success of this book.

I take pleasure in thanking the most beautiful eyes ever seen for the endless inspirations.

Preface

Poetry encompasses several definitions while it embraces unexpected and expected thoughts universally shared. The theme behind this anthology is mellow sexy which is a unique genre of poetry birthed by yours sincerely.

Mellexy began as a soft expression of feelings in a contemporary way. It is like a song best appreciated when read. Mellexy embraces a dimension of poetry for a soulful adventure and experience. The word mellexy is a delightful mix of mellow and sexy – Mellexy.

Mellexy is a unique genre of poetry, which is usually a short piece of sensuous and sensual poem that appeals to the feelings of the heart. It captures and evokes powerful emotions.

In summary, it is short piece of poetry that express endless feelings of emotions.

In the coming pages of this book, written poetry is featured for the pleasures of the heart. These poems share delightful blends of words in a manner to better express a feeling.

TABLE OF CONTENTS

INTRODUCTION

The human eye is one of the most remarkable features in the body. While it functions like the lens of a camera, it can distinguish between light and darkness. The eyes create images for our brains to comprehend out of light.

Pictures they say, speak a thousand words. With the eyes, you can have a memory bank of moving pictures without sound. The eyes don't lie. What you see is what you conceive. It reminds us of our past with what we have seen. More so, it helps us to embrace what we long to see in the future.

What do you see when you look in the eyes of the one you love? What do they see when they look into yours? Rhetorical.

Through the eyes, you can unlock the mystery of love. Does the phrase 'love at first sight' ring a bell? In a quest to understand why the eyes are so special, think about how we share our feelings with that special one. Letters are beautiful, a text is lovely, a face to face conversation is just about it, but an eye to eye conversation is another realm of its own.

As creatures of love, we want to express ourselves in as many ways as possible to others' understanding.

Through your eyes is a literary piece about the feeling of happiness, love and all that entails a refreshing joy. This literary work has an enjoyable taste as its narrative lies in the beauty of love in the eyes. This contemporary work is light-hearted. It revolves around fantasies and fiction, although it is very relatable as it evokes unspoken feelings and interpretations of intimate moments of what the eyes are saying.

It is written to be read **through your eyes** in the point of view as though the reader is the writer telling a tale about the love of your life.

A Tale In Your Eyes

I perished in the beauty of your eyes

As I lay on the ambient of your waters

In my dreams

I could only wish for a reality that you'll look at me

With sincerity that I'm yours

No deceit

No facade

In the silence of trust

I'm helplessly soaked in your glow like aurora

Gazing upon you like the stars

Made a wish that you'll finally see me

I bought a book

It's empty as my heart thirst for you

Hand me your pen

So we can write our stories

Every chapter will be blissful

With happy endings as a fairytale

We will be legends of bedtime stories

Help my heart with your love cure

Let your pure love divine fill me up

Through your eyes I see a destination

Take me there

Written to the one who seeks love and recklessly goes for it. Tell the one all you ever want, your dreams and aspirations. Kill the fantasy and break the ice. Let your intentions be known. Let the one your heart yearns for know your true feeling.

A tale in your eyes explores unspoken words like a story. It draws out the love essence from the eyes of my lover. While it is a fantasy of a love yet to be born. It is narrated as a letter of intent to evoke the feelings of my heart. This is the link bridge of fantasy to reality where the aim is to actualise every dream of my love fantasy.

Although it is a dream conceived out of a deep feeling too good to be true. The reality of this truth as always been right in front of me. I don't have to look any further for the wave of love lies in your eyes. You brought me into context with all that you are as you look through your eyes. Your eyes blow kisses for me to grab. Love on a cruise to endless happiness is all I see in your eyes.

It's like a feeling of visiting a new city on a wanderlust happy in blue. Visions of predestined adventures I have conceived. All that's left is for me to experience this feeling.

Come through, Come true ...

Bright Eyes

I woke up in your arms

Spooned in your warm embosom

Your heart beat I listen to keenly

Makes me feel safe and calm

Your soft breath at my ear lobe

tickles in a sweet fashionable way

I wear your aura with a smile

Beautiful and free

I get lost in your dazzling eyes

A spiral way to unlimited happiness

Shine on me everyday

Never blink

For I don't want to miss any moment

It is a whole universe in there

I see your stars

I want your light

My dying wish is to be in your arms

Gazing at those precious pearls

Till I fall asleep

praying to be healed by your kiss

In admiration of wholeness in the hands of a special one. Let the one you love know how much you appreciate their presence. It is a soothing relief of being in the comfort of love.

With the birth of newfound love, Bright eyes is a reality where love meets the eye. It snaps me out of fantasy to be in the reality of my dreams. A perfect dream that never fades away. In every dream, you wake up but in here it is a dream I wake up to. Sweetness in the arms of love divine as Bright Eyes is bliss in blue.

A eulogy to your graceful eyes and raw love with no filters. A living love set to keep me awake in my dreams. Waking up to you is like a healing rain to keep the roses of our love to bloom everlasting. You are the highlight of my life like the silver moon at night. The light in your eyes is like the sun, a consuming fire with pure energy set to burn till infinity.

In your flames cleanse me to purity. Let your beautiful eyes set on me every day. In my wake or my dream it doesn't matter where.

The Glow in Your Eyes

It shreds the darkness installed in me

Deactivates my indecisiveness

Draws me in like an artist

Telling a story in paintings

Your eyes

Sainted with a halo

Flourished with the scents of purity

The tiara in your eyes is worthy of every long gaze

Blessed by your look

Beamed into your world

Frozen by your milky touch

In a glance

You fix my broken glass

My world is whole again

You complete me

This is a welcoming love that makes everything alright. It is a healing love that fixes all with just a glance. Everyone deserves to feel special and be looked upon in admiration.

When the world is caving in and getting dark just a look into your eyes is enough to clear the thick fog of life. You invoke powers that take away my melancholy when I am with you.

You are happiness personified. Your glow is like a perfect lullaby soothing and calming. Your love is an alibi to take me through dark days. An avenue ever new to relief days strain. Your love is a lighthouse to guide me if I ever lose my way.

In admiration of your grace, 'The glow in your eyes' captures the light you emit like lights from a star light-years away that beautifies the universe and claims its existence. The existence of your love radiates further into my being which makes me beautiful. Through my eyes, the whole world can see all that I see.

You...

For My Eyes Only

My circuit burnt

as I gazed into your eyes

My configurations malfunctioned

as I watched your smile

draw up on your cheek

I died lively in your eyes

Paralyzed by your sight

You're my art

A portrait for my ardour

You deliver me from the snares of lost

I walk in grim valleys

with your halo hovering over my head

Let me into your secret

Hush me with a kiss

Your sensation I desire

Your bliss I testify

It's a tale scripted like an anthem

Wrapped in a ribbon like a scroll

Clandestine

For my eyes only

For a modicum time with your love in trust. Expressing the details in the beauty in their eyes as it lures your desires to be fully immersed the expression of love.

This revolves about a love reserved for my lover while it expresses in details the feelings it invokes. This feeling of love is not to be shared with anyone but confined in trust for our precious love. It is engraved in our heart never to be discarded.

This feeling is like the space between the sky and the ocean. It's a force of attraction like gravity that I can't let go but it keeps me in balance. I get this feeling only when I look into your eyes. It's an adventure floating like a feather, tender and beautiful. To be one with the wind, the sun, the moon and the star. This is the evolution of our love.

You invoke the true colours of love as I give you all of my expressions. My senses come alive when you look into my eyes. You make me linger for more under the veil.

You are the music in me. You turn my feeling on like hot weather. Through your eyes, let's watch our emotions dance with love like watching a ballerina perform on stage in elegance. At the balcony of my heart, you serenade me in your charm.

You opened my eyes to see the secrets you unfold like a rose in bloom. Your love flows through my vein for all of me belongs to you.

Something About Your Eyes

Your eyes are like the hills

It got me looking high

Show me your secrets

Let me unravel you

***

Your eyes are like the oceans

It got me surfing on your waves

Take me into your deep

Till I can finally breathe

***

Your eyes are like the stars

Through you I could see the universe

Reveal your hidden mystery

Let your evolving aura linger on me

***

Your eyes are like fire

It stirs up my burning desire

Purify me in your flames

Saint me with your love

***

Your eyes are like the wind

Blow me away with your precious petals

Pollinate my existence with your touch

Let me blossom in your fragrance

***

Your eyes are like pearls

Make me glitter like sapphires

Keep me in your sacred chest

Let all of me belong to you

Dedicated to a true love like a hymn. It sings praises of adoration to your lover. It describes the reflective feeling of love from the eyes of your lover.

This describes the unexplainable feeling I get whenever you look into my eyes. You reflect unspoken feelings of comfort, peace and satisfaction. While it proceeds to elate and paint a picture of a perfect reality by expressing the beauty in the eyes of my love. "Something About" your eyes satisfies the answer to describe the beauty in the eyes of my love.

Something about your eyes travels to explain further this line in ***For My Eyes Only***

- I died lively in your eyes

This oxymoron is about dreaming in a dream about the beauty in your eyes. Yet I am awake but helplessly marvelled by the aura you evoke. The feeling is like a wave from the ocean that washes and cools my feet.

It washes away the darkness as I look into your eyes. It's like a magnetic force that pulls me underneath. Your eyes took me out of the boundaries of my mind. To lay in a place with unlimited happiness. You make everything okay as you hold me with your eyes.

In My Reach

My feelings are on the high

When I'm with you

I try to keep my composure

Listening to what your eyes say

When you look at me

You stimulate me with a 5-star comfort

Daisies and roses

Fine and wine

With an ambience of the country side

Layered with wild bouquet of lavender

Your gentle love is flawless on my skin

The touch from your eyes

Makes me want you mentally and physically

Take care of me

Let me gaze into your eyes all day

And fall asleep in the beauty of your sphere

Let me belong to you

Holding onto you like tomorrow

Bless me in your celestial embrace

As you came my way with your love

Stay and lay by my side

I need you in my reach

For a longing to be in the arms of your love. The closer, the deeper the bond.

"In my reach" is a reminder of experience with my love. It about yearning for the company of my love. It's a lingering sensation which echoes to relive the time spent together.

I crave you to be closer, never out of sight, never out of touch. Wherever you are I want to feel your presence. Your voice is a healing spring. I have tasted your words. Now I crave you much more. Your love is like a happy ending in fairy tales. Keep in the loop of this feeling till infinity.

Watching You

With my eyes all over you

Absorbing every detail of your light

Unravelling the mystery of your charm

You're like a song

I have chosen to listen on repeat

You are easy on the eyes

Satisfying and pleasing

Like a memory on the wall

Seasonal like the fall

You are worth every gaze

like a planetary alignment

Patiently, pleasantly, preciously guarding you

like a relic of ancient past

In your details

Tales are twisted like lace

Every stroke of colour in your world

Echoes your elegance allure

Written to adore the feminine touch. In appreciation of the pleasures she evokes.

Admiring the beauty of my soul lover is a thrill like a holiday. ''Watching You' gives a pleasing light of ambience in describing my lover in adoration. It is a love here to stay. Its core focus is on your light which is my devotion to protecting. I dare not look away never to miss out on your pretty thoughts.

All of your secrets I have seen for it is as beautiful as the mystical city of Atlantis. You are a perfect creation to be adored. Your presence whispers your alluring grace. Every move you make is like the best scene in a romance novel. The way your eyes touched my skin caught me in thoughts of giving you all of my love.

Ice in My Eyes

To the ice in my eyes

You cool off my blues

with your wild smile

A wild card to reset my dark days

Rescue me into your light

Bless me with the sight of your smile

Let me live in the grace of your happy harvest

Share your fruit of poise

Let me sway

In your way

Pull up in your swag

You're such a delight

Keep shining

Let the world feel your warmth as it spreads over the horizon

All with just a cheek draw

Let your smile burst like a pouring rain.

Smile on me

You are my gem

An appreciation message to adore your lover.

This is a delightful praise to appreciate the love you evoke as it radiates like the ray of the sun. You are a blessing to everything you touch. You make forever at the moment you touched me. Since I found myself in you it has been easier to breathe. I feel the urge to appreciate you with this growing feeling too strong alone to bear. But with you, it becomes easier because you love simple.

With you, I am always winning as we sail through every ocean with ease. You gave my soul hope and purpose with love. You took away my fear and despair. My spirit is free to fly away to a brighter place and my road is no longer lonely for you are with me.

My mysteries, a misery to find a love divine was found with you. Since you rescued me with your light I never want to miss a moment with you. You are priceless and won't be traded for anything in the universe. My devotion is to keep you safe and protect your light. I stand by this.

Poetry in My Eyes

Let me touch you with my eyes

Let it linger on you

Watch as it draws you out of the water

Breathe a new air

Let the words that dance

Make you feel alive

Taking chances

Making you mine

Speaking without words to your understanding

Let my eyes do what hands do

Touching you to relax

Unwind your mind

Watch the moonlight in my eyes

as it reflects your colours

All that you are

Is all that I need

Let me pour my feelings on you

Till it reflects all of me

The sunset in your eyes

Compliments all of me

Meet me half way

Let me take you to the finish line

Your search for the thrill ends here

As I make you mine

Written for a muse.

You are like a walking poetry. Pleasant and graceful radiance of love expression you evoke. Your aura makes me feel special. You are like the notes on a keyboard. A sweet tone to the tune of love. You make me yearn to make delightful music with you.

You are like a picnic treat to the eyes. You explore my thought of expression effortlessly. You are the place I desire to hang all of my expressions on the wall of your beautiful mind.

My Wild

The look in your eyes

Paralyzed my unfold

My vulnerability is all for you to explore

Your skin is a discovery

Electrifying and silky

With every touch

You dissolve my melancholy in your ambiance

Burnt my resolve

Graced by your flame

Purified with your kiss

Sainted by the taste of your lips

Cleansed in your wild embrace

You don't have to say a word

Just a smile

And

I'm yours forever

An expression of emotions sanctified by the look from the eyes of your lover.

Expresses a reckless surrender to submit all of my love to you without worrying about a derail. You heal my melancholy with your touch on my life. When I am with you I feel a rush, I feel my soul yearning for your love.

Life is beautiful with you. Living in a world without you would be meaningless. My world would be in thick darkness without the presence of the sun and the moon. You are my sun at day and my moon at night.

Through your eyes you light up my existence and take away the dark. Your love is set to linger on me till the end of time. Since you came into my life you rain on me sweet memories that bring me joy.

The proceeds of your love is pure happiness which brings me gladness. Every day you mirror a future that reflects a world of uphill climbing. I can proudly say with all conviction that I am destined to be with you.

What I See In You?

I see many things in you

Maybe it's in my mind

Maybe I'm assuming

I look at you

I see love and honesty ready to be harvested

You've planted it all for the one to harvest

But you scared it will burn to the ground

Leaving you empty

Yet, you hopeful

Let me put you on top

Hold you close and raise you up proudly

Call you mine

And claim you to the world

A heart felt message to clarify any doubt about love while assuring your lover pure intentions.

A message to assure my love sincere and pure intentions. No deceit, no facade, no fear. Although, love could be a dangerous adventure for the heart. It is the purest of energy to make me feel alive.

It is lovely to be in love with you. Let me take your hand as I lead you into glee and bliss. I promise to make the wish on your lips come true with an eternal love.

Come Here

Come a little closer

Let me see your mind

Let me help you unwind

Head in my direction

Let me decipher your creation

To make sense of what you are

Till I figure all that you are

Let me dive into your eyes

Let me see through you

My curiosity won't let me breathe

Unconsciously swaying to your beat

I want to see the world through you

For your imagination is different

Watching you unfold is like a present

Pull me underneath your cloak

Let's paint a future with our eyes

In awe of a beautiful creation.

"Come here" conveys a message about my love beyond the surface. There is so much beauty to unravel within you. You are like a stacking doll with different layers of blessings, grace, elegance, happiness and the finest of thoughts.

Every day you grow more amazing. Your intriguing attribute draws me closer to you. I eagerly want to spend my days and time with you. You took my fears away and brought me into you light.

All that's left is to forge a future with you. With hope to make the world a better place. Even if it takes many nights or 100 years. I am destined to end up in this place with you.

Transparent

All my life I searched

Just to realize

That all I ever wanted is in your eyes

Those daring eyes capable of swallowing an ocean

You filtered the debris from life

Then dissolved my heart in your water

A perfect solution

Clear and pure

like water

You are the perfect solvent

We blend uniformly

Through your eyes

I see the world differently

Transparent and safe

For a conceived and perceived thought of your love.

A love that takes you on a journey on true discovery. To see the plains of the heart, hikes on the mountains of desires and deep into the ocean of affection. Without having to imagine what love is, you make me see it all. To perceive your true intentions.

My Dream

Your love of many colours I wear

Proudly

In this fantasy

It is plain to see

Your love divine

My rainbow in the sun

You sheltered my heart

And gave this love a home

I found my wild in you

Clear as crystal

I am living my dream with you

My reality

You are true to me

For a reality like a dream. Living in a dream that is vivid and real.

Through your eyes I can see expectations of this love. I saw how far we have come and where it would take us. We both know how this would end. Just the way you expected, spending the rest of our lives together in bliss.

New Moon

The curve in your eyes is fresh like a new moon

As it faints into the twilight

It reminds me of song

You

My song, my melody, my symphony

The way your eyes opens like a rose in the summer

Sprouts an irresistible feeling like a fragrance in spring

You are my constant

My season with eternal harvest

As I bask in bewilderment of your precious sight

I trade everything I've got to be with you

Just to be in your soft light

As you wear the night elegantly

Spreading your shade

Filtering the noise to disperse joy

The euphoria of your presence

Makes everything alright

All I want is to be wrapped like gift in your arms

Under your sterile gaze

A message of gratitude to your love. To appreciate the love you have found.

You are my season, rain and sunshine. You brought me out of darkness into your light. You are my favourite discovery. The one I want to give all of my love.

Together forever I know you are the one. The one my heart chose.

The love I craved all my life. I found when I looked into your eyes.

You inspire me with your beauty divine - internally and externally.

Let your light fall and soak me in deep.

As you came my way with your love. You came in and stayed with

your presence – physically, mentally and emotionally. Whenever I

took into your eyes I yearn to always have you in my reach. As days

goes by, as night covers the surface, as seasons change my love for

you never alters.

You Are a Feeling

Charge to my rescue

For I'm phasing out of emotions

I hear your sound approaching in distant

like footsteps from the hollowed hallway

The tingling sensation of your voice

Arouses my subconscious

Bring me to life

I'm anticipating

Like the rising morning sun

Your presence arrays a red carpet

I crave for you to walk into my heart

Bathe me in your warmth once again

Stay with me and never let me go

A personification of your lover whose appearance and nature is more than the physical but transcends mentally and emotionally.

Your love took me higher than I have ever felt before. You make my world shine in new colours. You come with a feeling like a dream in blue. Let me uncover all of your truth.

The feelings you invoke undresses my mind to the thought of you. You propel a desire to house my heart in a new home with you. No one else sees me the way you do. Nothing can compare to the feeling you latch on me.

In Your Hue

I fell into your orbit

Like the planetary bodies

My thoughts revolves around you

You are my irreplaceable sun

I see your shadows in my room

My subconscious creates your construct in my sleep

Hold me close

Let the rays from eyes comfort me

Serenade me in your warmth

Your presence is a sweet lullaby

As it undresses my mind

Envelope my heart with your message

Let it massage my melancholy to blue

In your hue

I see you in true

Plain and naked

Recklessly giving your all to me

Making it clear

That you'll be here when I wake

An assurance of a love here to stay.

Nothing more, nothing less than a beautiful view is your sight. You are a beautiful scene in my dream. My reality in bloom like a rainbow with a sign. A promise of love divinely destined and entwined with time.

We are closely knitted into one like braided cords. Your love converge to take a shape in my heart. We unravel, twist and connect at every turn in time. My reality and dream are the same for I am blessed to be loved by you.

Electric

I feel your energy running through my nerves

Your sensation satisfies my core

Let me wear your sparkle like a crown

In my static state

I'm naked in thoughts

Latch onto me

See that all of me is for you

Watch me strip my feelings

And discover my passion for you

Touch me

Let your touch take me away

Watch my heart race for you

Power my core with your kiss

Look into the depth of my heart

Hold me like it's the last time

And never let go

For the paradise in your arms

Is perfect like the music of our heart beats

A powerful feeling that gives light and energy to the soul.

Everything I want in love I've found. Patience, peace and protection. In my dreams I see flashes of you as I picture the future ahead of us. Seeing the life we are going to live. I can't imagine a world without you. I need your touch to fuel me. You are my energy, you are my spark.

In your glam, life is sweet like vanilla. Light of my life, light up my eyes. Airdrop your safety net to my heart.

My Sunset

You awash at the plains of my life

With a true meaning

I see you rise like a silhouette

Absorbing the rays of the falling golden sun

A goddess

Glowing in her gracious wake

Your colours

Something different I can't explain

My imaginations see you coming into existence

Wish I could skip this preview

As you head towards my direction

Your view

Comes into perspective

The perfect picture

Painted in my mind

Comes alive as you are

A perfect picture to paint the description of your lover.

As you are I will follow you to the end of the world. You are everything that I see. I am more of myself around you than when I am alone. I want all of your love and emotions as you set your light on me.

I have spent most of my life preparing my heart for you. Now I can catch my breath because it is so easy to be in love with you. Through your eyes I see beauty in everything.

My Crest

To my treasure and pride

You lavish my life with pure joy

When I'm with you

I fall to pieces

Like colourful confetti rain

You whitewash my soul

In your reflecting hue

You balance me like a fulcrum

You terraform my heart

With your lingering aura

You are the change I've been longing for

You came in to fill a void

All of my precious memories are with you

I sleep easy with you engraved on my heart

Every second feels like eternity with you

The ledge of your trust is a safe haven

Before I transcend from dust

I will defend our love till the end of time

A vow of love.

I will honour our love with diligence and respect. Protect it like it's the last source of light in the universe. You are my clarity, a day I look forward to. I feel your warmth with just the thought of you.

I pledge to protect the answer to my prayers. I will continue to fly the flag of our love to show the world my allegiance to you. The pleasure of loving you feels like heaven. I call you my angel because the light from your halo purifies my thoughts and being.

Peaches

Let me feel your heaven

Take me **on the path** to your rose garden

Convey me **into your inner world**

Let me **share your beautiful**

You are the missing piece to my wholeness

Sweetness divine **like vanilla** I promise

The more **I** see you

The more I **miss you**

You make my world feel **like a dream**

Perfect

...

You brighten me excessively like peaches **under the sun**

Like a lost chapter

I found myself with you

Running **across the water** to be with you

Caving all of my emotions into one essence

To express them **with you**

A secret message for your love.

"Let me on the path into your inner world to share your beauty. You are like vanilla. I miss you like a dream. Under the sun I found myself across the water with you."

Peaches is a bottle message for my love with promises of love bliss. It is a collision course of love. An explosive love like the big bang to create beautiful creations and memories. A world with you is glamourous where all my dreams are realised.

Rendezvous

You took me back to our tasteful beginning

Every day is freshly baked with you

You are refreshing like the waves from the beach

A love that doesn't age a day

Down the road of life

You took me into your secret world

A life like a movie

On a parallel ride, no roller coaster

Listening to our favourite song

In the muse of our company

You make it simple

As you remind me of the feeling

That rush feeling

Like we struck love like oil

Dreams of my breath stolen away

Came alive when I'm with you

A reminder of true love.

I still feel your kiss against my lips from the first time. A sweet memory I still miss. You take me back to this thought with every precious feeling you give to me.

As time passes by I can't help but to tell you how special you are. I can't put anyone above because I know and I've realised there is no one I can love like you.

I have had sleepless nights from missing you and the memories we have created. So I look forward to making more memories with you. To share memories we would sit and watch together. The only thing we'll ever see is a life of joy.

In the Awe of You

It seems I have been destined to end up in this place

With you laying on cloud of roses

Picnic in the sky

Soft focus on us

Floating in the garden with all we want

You and I in Eden

We cast ourselves like a movie

Premiere just for our eyes

In point of view your lips is all I see

Your voice is a sweet melody in my wake

Your gaze at me is worth more than lost treasures

Sought by bandits and pirates

Your flirting eyes drives me to desire you more

Take me into your bliss

Spiced with rosemary and thyme

Topped with strawberries to the taste of your grace

Lace me in your aura

Your fragrance creates ambience like a chandelier in a ball room

Take my hand

Let's dance till our legs go weary

For the night is ours

In bewilderment of a fascinating love.

When I close my eyes I see you in all of your grace. The smell of you in my dreams gladness my heart. You give this love a direction like a ray of sun. My body gets warmer whenever you close the gap between us.

You made this lonely heart fulfilled with a promise kept. You outline my life with the definition of love. No matter the season or weather I am always caught up in your heatwave. Spotlight of my life with the key to my heart. You cool me off from within.

Candy Rain

All my life

You rain down on me sweetness

Glances of you

Reflecting through the window

Like moon dapples

Marks your territory in my heart

You settled in

You gave me without taking

Your kiss stops me from quivering

It feels new every time

The only way for me

is to give you all of myself

Wrapped in your sweetness

Like fairy floss

All I ever needed in life

I found it in you

I don't have to dream of a candy rain

You're my cloud

For a sweet savouring taste of love.

With a love so true, you lay on me pleasantries as you serenade my eyes with your smile. There is no doubt, no second guess about you. You hover me with a reality I am pleased to have.

A sky full of colours in your hands. I feel your presence coming down like the night drawing nearer. Set me free with your touch. My daily rain of sweetness, soak me in your celestial bliss.

Fill Me In

Pull up in my mind

Show me your fantasy when you look at me

Let me in on a glimpse of you

Putting on that dress I like

Black satin and lace

Show me your clouds

Let it rain on me

Let your love down

Soak me in your velvet scents

Let me in to see your beautiful dream

Wrap me up in your thoughts

Show me your hide away

Show me what you see when you close your eyes

Fill me in on how our love makes you melt

Let your love run wild on me

Wake me up to fill me in on my curiosity

You don't have to say a word

Show me through your eyes

A message to your lover to reveal every enticing mystery.

Put on your slide show let me see it all. Take me on a journey into your mind. Let me watch you display at the balcony of your mind. Singing a lullaby telling a tale I can understand. I have seen glimpses now show me everything. My queen of the clouds I long for you to reveal what you see when your eyes are closed.

Noticing You

Noticing you shine like a star in the night

Let your light pour on me like the rains

Bless me with your soft filters

Pull me into your light

***

Noticing you shine like a diamond that you are

Let your reflection glitter on me

Your precious sight is framed in my heart

In bits and pieces I'm drawn to you

***

Noticing your eyes glow like a jelly fish in the dark

Your blue comes alive in ultraviolet light

Hold me in the dark

Let me share your cordial glow

***

Noticing your colours go green like foxfire

I yearn to your call to hold you back

And gaze into your eyes with alluring intentions

To lift you off the ground with a kiss

***

Noticing this feelings turn red as the night gets darker

Being by your side to fuel this thoughts

Feels better like a taste of wine as we connect

Till we unleash the hidden desires

In appreciation of the beauty your love evokes.

Every step I take with you, I appreciate your presence much more. I notice everything about you. You make everything that don't make sense about me make sense when I am with. You make me feel wanted with your love. You build me up and raise me up.

I notice how you carry your heart graciously, guarding and preciously. But you gave it all to me because you knew I would comfort you with a love so true. Look at what we are – we are like stars in the night glittering and shining.

Star Gazing

We are like dusts from the same star

A figment of the universe

A reflection as a nebula

A beautiful sight like Rigel in Orion

***

We are like a constellation telling a story

Your eyes are like a mirror that sees beyond the event horizon

Impossible is nothing before you

For we are connected to all of existence

***

We are like a binary star

You and I

At the center of it all

In stability among the stars

***

You are like a white dwarf star

Sterilize and cleanse me in your rays

Hold me in your gravity

Relay your celestial prowess on me

***

In the beauty of the night

You spread across the sky like ashes

I set my eyes on you in utter admiration

To immerse your luminosity

A hymn in adoration of love.

As it beautifully describes my love colourful as a rainbow. You are the core of my love. The birthplace of the existence of love. You made me believe in love.

As the planets revolves round the sun bathing in its light so does your love fuel and breathe life into my existence. Words alone can't comprehend the power of your love. The greatest gift to mankind is truly and indeed love but having you to share this love with is bliss.

As the expanding universe and its mysteries fascinates scientist and enthusiast of that field is the same way your love amazes and amuses me. This growing love is unique and different. There's nothing missing. All I have ever needed is in your love. I'll take my time to find, explore and marvel in the beauty of your love.

Oceans in Your Eyes

I drew from the rivers of your eyes

To heal the thirst in my heart

Your latches filtered the debris in my lonely soul

It is beautiful to love you

Watching the memories we created

Dance in the ball room of my mind

Under the floral chandelier

Raining daises and roses

As we find ourselves at every turn

Surfing on your love waves

To awash under the pines of your embrace

To be blessed by white sunlight

For I am openly proud to hold you close

And claim you to the world

A poem to openly embrace your lover.

"Oceans in your eyes" is a wandering adventure to discover what treasures lies in the beautiful eyes of my love. What secrets it beholds? While it uncovers this secret, Ocean in your eyes pictures the moment our love was born like a star. It follows its growth over time as it becomes stable with reference to memories we created together.

Your love healed my sad and depressing emotions. You are a feeling that shades away the grey and adds fruitful colours to my life.

The Muse in Your Eyes

Excuse the way I stare

For I am out of words to describe you

Let me savour in the moment

To capture your picture in my mind

My memory bank is rich with all shades of You

My eyes are stuck on you like a magnet

Now that I'm with you

I feel so much alive

Your touch feels like heaven

I can't take my eyes off you

With you by my side

Nights are warmer

Mornings are brighter

I'm speechless when I gaze helplessly into your pretty eyes

Trust me when I say

You are the answer to my prayers

I'll never let go off you

Like the clock I'll watch you every second

Sweetness

Let your love arrival peruse my reality

As you distilled the grey away

To fade in

To stay

You evoke pretty thoughts

I'm blessed to have you

A poem to express the stimulating pleasures of a vivid painting in the mind.

You channel endless inspirations when I look into your eyes. You drive my creativity into existence. In appreciation of my love, "The Muse in your eyes" describes my love as a happy place to be while it expresses comfort, safety and security. It comes with a prayer of thanks from my heart. You are all about beautiful thoughts packaged like a wrapped gift.

Your presence emits moments of peace and ambience. A look into your takes away misery and despair in a glance. Everything you do is effortless as I channel your positive aura through love emotions built up to make it alright. A life with you is a dream in bliss. People have searched but I found this with you. You are more than a fantasy, you are my reality.

You

You came along with a crimson smile

You work my mind with the thoughts

Precious thoughts of you

You light up like a stage

I see the angels through you

Your face is ever beautiful unto the new age

You channel the grace of the celestial

Your glowing face evolves with every look you give

Your smile is timeless

All we have is our souls entwined

Can you hear my heart scream?

The silent whisper only you can hear

You're the one

The one I reserved my feelings for

Let me be your left right

Let's get lost to the sound of our heart beat

Hold me as we dance to the rhythm

I found a perfect place with you

Where our love reflects on your face

Let's help each other escape

I have waited for all my life

For a promised tomorrow

The only truth I know

You are my tomorrow

I have been waiting for you

Written to adore your soulmate in a gracious way like an angel in the flesh.

"You" precisely defines the thoughts I have about my love. It comes

with a serenading touch with an ambience of a fantasy. It describes

a feeling of swimming in a heavenly ocean of love. Floating in the

grace of the power of my love. It lays emphasis on this line in **The**

Muse In Your Eyes

- My memory bank is rich with all shades of You

You are everything. Your love transcends beyond life. Your love is adequate with an energy that never burns out. A look in your eyes makes my senses feel more alive. You are the definition of my concept of love. You understand my love language without speaking for we are always in sync. A love that get newer every passing day is what I share with you.

Printed in Great Britain
by Amazon